# A Contemporary Portrait of the Southwest

# A Contemporary Portrait of the Southwest

Connor M. Bjotvedt

A Contemporary Portrait of the Southwest
Copyright © 2021 Connor M. Bjotvedt
All Rights Reserved.
Published by Unsolicited Press.
Printed in the United States of America.
First Edition.

No part of this book may be used or reproduced in any manner whatsoever without written permission except in the case of brief quotations embodied in critical articles or reviews. People, places, and notions in these stories are from the author's imagination; any resemblance is purely coincidental.

Attention schools and businesses: for discounted copies on large orders, please contact the publisher directly.

For information contact:
Unsolicited Press
Portland, Oregon
www.unsolicitedpress.com
orders@unsolicitedpress.com
619-354-8005

Cover Designer: Kathryn Gerhardt
Editor: Bekah Stogner


ISBN: 978-1-950730-85-8

# Table of Contents

| | |
|---|---|
| https://phoenix.jobing.com/bgcmp/faculty-studenteditor-part-time-1-9419122 | 9 |
| Article Submission: Faculty Editor 16/17 | 11 |
| RE: [A Contemporary Portrait of the Southwest] - Committee Approval - | 14 |
| New Order, New Marshall | 15 |
| Lawrence of Arizona | 16 |
| | |
| I | 19 |
| Last Man Standing | 20 |
| A Passenger Arriving at Sky Harbor | 22 |
| *The Jew and The Arab Ride on Deep into the Desert* – J Herr | 23 |
| My Rough Start | 24 |
| Separate but Equal | 25 |
| Precision, Precisely | 27 |
| "*Conservation of the Range*" – Michael Beckler | 28 |
| The Race to $22.50 | 29 |
| The Racing Circuit: A Business Servicing the Community | 30 |
| Dinner with the Mayor | 31 |
| In Medina, Do as the Medinan | 32 |
| "I've killed the Indian and built a white man in his place." – Rev. Thomas L. Moore | 34 |
| Percussion, Resonance | 36 |
| The Controversy Behind the New Fútbol Stadium | 37 |
| -Industry Partners- | 38 |
| Terraforma: (N) The Great Hill of Northern Arizona | 39 |

| | |
|---|---|
| Levity, Brevity | 40 |
| A Rational Discussion of the Phoenix Punk Rock Scene | 41 |
| Marketing 101 – Capital Investment Among Other Sorts | 43 |
| Horace B. Griffen Trust—Application for Financial Aid Disbursement | 45 |
| The Crippling Letter: Opportunism | 46 |
| The Crippling Letter: Opportunism | 47 |
| | |
| II | 49 |
| Organizers Weekend: Commercial Parity | 50 |
| "A Girl's Political Window" | 52 |
| Katherine's Law | 53 |
| The Franchise and the Franchisee | 54 |
| "*Ride-Sharing Litter*" – Jeff Whitehall | 55 |
| A Hippie in the Southwest | 56 |
| "Jerry might have liked to read what you've written." – Lois Jacka | 57 |
| Quality Control: "What is Water and where does it come from?" | 58 |
| Watering the Grass©: Fountain Hills, The Water Conservation Project | 60 |
| Watering the Grass©: Marching Orders | 61 |
| Watering the Grass©: Marching Orders | 62 |
| Watering the Grass©: The Conditional Surrender of Claim #46-01 | 63 |
| Watering the Grass©: Taken to Heart | 65 |
| Watering the Grass©: Taken to Heart | 66 |
| Watering the Grass©: Salting the Earth, Sport Replenishment in the Sub-Tropic | 67 |
| // [34.5769° N, 113.1764° W] | 68 |
| Local Traditions©: Make Sure You're Drinking Enough Water | 69 |
| Local Traditions©: Cactus Butter | 71 |

| | |
|---|---|
| Local Traditions©: [Redaction] Cactus Butter | 72 |
| My $20 Lunch with a Yuma County Sherriff | 73 |
| Dining in the Desert©: PBS Frontline Exclusive, "The Business of Food" | 74 |
| Dining in the Desert©: Finding Ways to Cook for Two | 76 |
| Dining in the Desert©: The Banquet Challenge | 77 |
| Dining in the Desert©: The Last Meal, or the Humanitarian Option | 78 |
| jw2293@utah.edu | 81 |
| About the Author | 83 |
| About the Press | 84 |

# https://phoenix.jobing.com/bgcmp/faculty-studenteditor-part-time-1-9419122

*The Arizona Get-a-way*

Faculty / Student Editor – Part-time

Pay: $22.50/hr
Posted: 5-5-2016
Status: Part-time

Job Description:

Job Summary:

Click here to submit to CACC

Applicants should be prepared to engage, challenge, and nurture our students and faculty over the course of a three (3) month residency which they will complete at Central Arizona Community College in Coolidge, Arizona. Applicants should be prepared to teach students how to demonstrate competent written techniques in the art of Journalism and should prepare themselves to oversee the publication of our bi-monthly student journal, *The Arizona Get-a-way*. <u>Applicants should familiarize themselves with our library of previous publications before submitting</u>.

Major Responsibilities:

- Candidates must be willing to pursue promotional contracts and sponsorships which are in accordance with the *Get-a-way's* corporate image, core-beliefs, &values.
- Candidates must be willing to submit timely or otherwise contemporary op-eds which speak to the on-goings of our city and our state.
- Candidates must be willing to oversee the *Get-a-way's* day-to-day operations and must be comfortable fielding questions from students and faculty.
- Candidates will follow our production schedule: Candidates will collect student editorials no less than three (3) weeks before publication deadlines.
- Candidates will teach: Candidates are required to develop and administer two (2) summer courses which *acknowledge* the art of journalism.

Skills and Requirements:

-Applicants should be comfortable in crowded areas and should be comfortable speaking to large groups of students and colleagues.
-Applicants should be familiar with the commitments of an editorial position.
-Applicants should be able to manage a sizable production staff.
-Applicants should be up to date on all current publishing standards.

Qualifications:

-Advanced college degree or relevant/ equivalent work experience.

Click here to submit to CACC

# Article Submission: Faculty Editor 16/17
Sub: Applicant, John Ryan Whenn [Lake Havasu City, Az]

7 attachments (501kb)        Download all        Save all to OneDrive – U of U


Dear Ryan Hill,

Hello, my name is John Ryan Whenn. I was born and raised in Lake Havasu City, AZ. I was educated at the Walter Cronkite School of Journalism and Mass Communication at Arizona State University. I received a Master of Fine Arts in Writing from Vermont College and completed 6 course hours of Doctoral studies at the University of Utah.

I have previously worked for The State Press, Hunger Mountain, and the Salt Lake Tribune. Attached you will find my 3 letters of recommendation, my official transcripts, a 10-page writing sample, and below, you will find my morning's ritual—an experiment in my form.

Cheers, and happy hunting.

John Ryan Whenn


### A Contemporary Portrait of the Southwest
"What does it mean to balance a budget?"

"Throughout the coming weeks, county administrators and city officials will begin to withdraw their extracurricular financing in an effort to balance our city's budgetary deficit; for our *annual* members, that means that until further notice all courses, workshops, and exercise programs will be canceled or rescheduled in regards to our teacher's commitment and availability." – Jessica Harper, Tucson City Parks

"Community centers, courses, and leagues across the nation are facing budgetary restraints and depletion in the wake of runaway inflation and the establishment of a universal health care program; states, like ours, who were ill-equipped to handle a devastating financial obligation, like a universal health care system, have been forced to cut nearly 90% of their community outreach programming and as a result have endangered or damaged the lives of thousands of at risk or soon to be at risk teens and children." (w/ *Coppertone Basin*)

"Taxes remain at an all-time low in the desert state, a *triumph* for commercial businesses and industries, however, many young legislators are working to change that. In November, Arizona Democrats are hoping to pass new regulations which would bring 'taxation into the 21$^{st}$ century;' The proposition, dubbed '*From the Ashes*,' plans to raise the state's single filer's burden to 16.5%, and plans to impose levies as high as 52% on earners of at least $500,000, or more. The bill's *progressive* caucus heralds their *stimulus* as nothing short of a modern-day miracle, but for those whom the bill targets it represents financial Armageddon." (w/ Fox12)

# RE: [A Contemporary Portrait of the Southwest] -
### Committee Approval -
Applicant J.R. Whenn; Lake Havasu City, Arizona

Dear John,

My committee was impressed by your work's provocative and surrealistic attempts to contemporize the day-to-day on-goings of the southwest; aesthetically, your pieces are rather unique and unlike anything we've seen or currently publish. The *collage* is not something we normally consider to be an *appropriate* form for editorial pieces; however, your work's humor and blunt certainty has charmed our staff into making an exception.

Currently, we are comfortable with offering you the following position:

>[Adjunct, Junior-Faculty]
>Central Arizona Community College:
>College of Journalism
>[Term]
>Summer (June, July, August)

We appreciate your patience
and are incredibly eager to present you to our students
and our faculty.

Please contact your department chair, ALLEN POWER,
at (480) 511-1988, or online at **allenp@centralaz.edu**,
with any questions or concerns you might have surrounding your residency.

Thank you and welcome to the team,
Ryan Hill
Dir. of Student and Faculty Orientation

# New Order, New Marshall

Sub: Hello—Allen, I'm John.

4 attachments (187kb)   Download all   Save all to OneDrive - CACC

Allen,

Hello, my name is John. I was told to contact you by the orientation office; I'm your new hire.

I believe that Ryan intended for me to provide you with a brief introduction to my work, so I'll oblige him; Allen, you will see shortly that my editorials do not seek to comply with any received form, but rather represent a careful study of post-modern literature and contemporary poetics. My work can be classified as experimental— although your hiring office seemed to appreciate it for its humor and blunt terseness.

I am eager to get to work on this summer's upcoming issues. The season's theme is still *Agency* in the Southwest, correct? Or has it changed? I've written a few pieces in preparation for that topic. I'll send them along as attachments to this e-mail. It is such a pleasure to be able to work for a periodical again—I can't express to you how truly excited I am.

Cheers,

John


John Ryan Whenn
*Arizona Get-a-way Junior, Faculty Editor*
Central Arizona Community College
jrwhenn@centralaz.edu

# Lawrence of Arizona

Sub: Hello John—Thank You for Your Introduction. Please Complete Your Employee Registration

**Employee Name:** John R. Whenn               **Employee ID:** 002965468

**Department:** Journalism                     **Date of Hire:** 4/12/2017

**Position:** Adjunct Lecturer/ Junior, Faculty Editor and Columnist

**Contract Length:** Summer 16/17

**Home Address:**          **City:**          **State:** AZ  **Zip Code:**

**Birth Date:**            **Marital Status:**  **Nationality/ Legal Status:**

Allen Michael Power
Journalism Department Chair
Central Arizona Community College
allenp@centralaz.edu

---

# Lawrence of Arizona

Re: Hello John—Thank You for Your Introduction. Please Complete Your Employee Registration

**Employee Name:** John Ryan Whenn             **Employee ID:** 002965468

**Department:** Journalism                     **Date of Hire:** 4/12/2017

**Position:** Adjunct Lecturer/ Junior, Faculty Editor and Columnist

**Contract Length:** Summer 16/17

**Home Address:** 1070 N 8th Pl   **City:** Coolidge
**State:** AZ   **Zip Code:** 85128

**Birth Date:** 04/29/1986  **Marital Status:** Single
**Nationality/ Legal Status**: US, Citizen


John Ryan Whenn
*Arizona Get-a-way Junior, Faculty Editor*
Central Arizona Community College
jrwhenn@centralaz.edu

I

# Last Man Standing
Sub: Publishing Goals for Summer 16/17

John,

Ryan went above my head when he *conscripted* you into my press corps. I am not happy with his decision—unlike him, I'm unsold on your rather *unique* editorialization; so, before we *'get to it'* and begin our summer on the wrong foot, I believe it's important for me to *'lay the ground rules,'* or, in-essence, instruct you on how I expect you to perform your role:

1. First, it is my hope that the work which you and your students produce this summer will draw attention to the various forms of injustice which currently *plague* the state of Arizona.
2. Second, it is my hope that you will address the historical aspects of this mistreatment and probe this *his·to·ry* in order to explore its varied political and socio-economic complexity.
3. Third, it is my hope that you will address the issues surrounding resource allocation and resource management within the state of Arizona; who goes with and without our resources?

4. Fourth, it is my hope that you will discuss the various enterprising businesses and markets which have emerged in our *ever-modernizing* part of the world.
5. Finally, it is Ryan's hope that your work will maintain its *humor* and *inventive* displays of literary engagement, yet it is my hope that your work will correctly produce a *contemporary* portrait of the Arizonan people, landscape, and culture.

Good Luck,

Allen


Allen Michael Power
Journalism Department Chair
Central Arizona Community College
allenp@centralaz.edu

# A Passenger Arriving at Sky Harbor
John's Travel Notes: An Introductory Course to the Phoenix Sky Harbor International Airport

A passenger arriving at Sky Harbor should remember to undress themselves as quickly as possible once they've landed. I've wasted a great portion of my day wandering around this airport and I've noticed that the preferred *dress* for this part of the world seems to be a mixture of panties and torn tee-shirts. Now, I don't know if this *evidence* denotes a change in the travel industry or if it's simply just a reflection of our local culture—but in either case, I believe this is my first *true* glance of the Southwest and I must say, "I rather like it here."

## *The Jew and The Arab Ride on Deep into the Desert* – J Herr
John's Travel Notes: An Introductory Course to the Scottsdale Museum of Contemporary Art

I don't think I'm a fan of contemporary art, but I believe
I have a new appreciation for the artist J Herr.
From what I've heard, he doesn't make much of an effort
to explain himself or his work, but there is a definite humor
about it which I appreciate.

> "There's a humor about it, which I appreciate; the artist depicts the two figures, the Jew and the Arab, riding together towards vacancy. He implies that they are choosing to say nothing to one another. He implies that they are simply choosing to exist in the presence of that moment. Herr brings the two, the Jew and the Arab, together on an *ass's* back and pressures them into foregoing their heritages and their hate: Herr allows these men to exist as themselves— alone, in this silent moment."—SMoCA Docent, Michelle Báách

# My Rough Start
Sub: [Priority Assignment] The American Concentration Camp -(1)-


John,

I understand that the temptation to simply define the southwest by its unique & *eccentric* qualities is rather overwhelming; however, that is not what I've asked you to do. In your pieces "A Passenger Arriving at Sky Harbor" and "The Jew and The Arab Ride on Deep into the Desert," I see a complicated relationship forming between your subject and your perspective; moving forward, I urge you to distance yourself from your work—this is not creative writing. Your perspective does not imbue your work with *some* surplus of authorial credibility. In fact, your *personal-touch* may lead the reader to assume that a colonizing, *tonal* bias has impregnated the pages of our publication.

John,

~~In order to tame the conflicts arising between yourself and I,~~ I think you should focus on new topics: I suggest you consider drafting a piece which would examine our state's internment camps. I urge you to stick to the facts and to focus on their inalienable, *historic* qualities. John, do not portray the events—report them. I'm not paying you to maintain a curious mind.

Good luck,

Allen.


Allen Michael Power
Journalism Department Chair
Central Arizona Community College
allenp@centralaz.edu

## Separate but Equal
Re: [Priority Assignment] The American Concentration Camp -(2)-

Allen,

This is an incredibly somber topic.
I didn't expect to be assigned
to something like this so quickly.

Please give me a moment to gather my thoughts.

John Ryan Whenn
*Arizona Get-a-way Junior, Faculty Editor*
Central Arizona Community College
jrwhenn@centralaz.edu

---

## Separate but Equal
Re: [Priority Assignment] The American Concentration Camp -(3)-

Allen,

This is what I've been able to piece together so far:

- The Gila River and Colorado River Internment Camps housed 31,000 Japanese Americans during the United States' campaign in the Pacific.
- These camps did not house political prisoners nor active combatants; These camps housed naturalized citizens and Japanese immigrants who faced extreme persecution and segregation after the bombing of Pearl Harbor.

- These camps were constructed inside the Gila River and Colorado River Indian Reservations; These camps were constructed on confiscated and appropriated land. These camps violated federal land trust agreements and infringed on the sovereignty of two nations.

- These camps maintained high enough populations to be considered the 3rd and 4th most inhabited cities within the state of Arizona.

- These camps and 8 others contributed to the death of 1,800 incarcerated Americans.

- These camps did not impact the war.

John Ryan Whenn
*Arizona Get-a-way Junior, Faculty Editor*
Central Arizona Community College
jrwhenn@centralaz.edu

# Precision, Precisely

Re: [Priority Assignment] The American Concentration Camp -(4)-

John,

I believe that your last piece was truly, refreshingly concise and that it was genuinely, unforgivingly concerned with the facts and finalities of the horrible and atrocious treatment of our nation's Japanese Americans. I believe that if you choose to continue to report on your interests and your assignments in this manner, then you will produce a quality of work which is unmatched by any traveling editor we have ever hosted—or any editor who is currently publishing in our dear city.

John,

I believe you possess a unique talent for editorializing events, however, our publication has no interest in stories; your many years of creative writing lessons will do you no good here.

John,

It would do you well to reflect on your life and to understand the privileges that you've been afforded, because you will receive none of them from me.

Good luck with the rest of the semester,

Allen.


Allen Michael Power
Journalism Department Chair
Central Arizona Community College
allenp@centralaz.edu

# "*Conservation of the Range*" — Michael Beckler
The Valley Conservative

"Even in our modern age, ranchers and motorists of the Central Valley are still at risk of colliding physically and financially with our largest, reintroduced, wild specimen: the horse." (w/ *A-Z Story-Hour*)

"Reintroduced to the southwest by Spanish missionaries, the horse quickly reestablished itself as the dominant herbivore in the vastly complicated desert food chain." — Bryan Doyer (ASU Fac.)

"Capitalizing off its size and lack of any natural predators, the horse soon took over the desert and drove out its competitors. For 500 years the horse has dominated and scavenged the west. . ."

". . . and this domination does not seem to be ending anytime soon. With the introduction of House Bill 2340, the horse will have finally left its last wild mark on the people and the landscape that it has lorded over." (w/ The Valley Conservative)

"Under the new bill, the horse will be officially classified as an endemic-non-invasive-species—and will be protected from poaching and harassment on all national parks and land. The *horse* has finally won the west." (w/ The Southwestern Equine)

# The Race to $22.50
The Arizona Teachers March

"After losing a significant margin of local purchasing power to the minimum wage increase, the Arizona teacher's union mobilized and organized a walk-out in an attempt to secure a *competitive* wage increase for all their districts and employees."
(w/ Arizona Board of Education)

"To drum up support for their march, the teachers compared their living expenses and wages to those of fellow Southwestern states. For three months, protestors urged parents and voters to view the state's-*new millennium*-spending as, '*grand larceny & theft*.' which was later substantiated by a state audit which found, '*numerous attempts to defraud the public schools.*'" (w/ *Family Matters*)

"The union's stand was met with initial praise and community support and continued to receive that support even in the face of a complete rejection of Doug Ducey's revised budget and educational package; which, to them, seemed to only target teacher's salaries."
(w/ The Valley Sun)

"The revised budget neglected both hourly workers and '*inflation-adjusted* student spending. The plan did not provide schools with the surplus funds needed to perform necessary building maintenance, nor did it provide additional capital to establish more advanced *after-school* programs. To them, Ducey's plan represented the worst qualities of capital government: self-service and individual compromise ." (w/Red)

# The Racing Circuit: A Business Servicing the Community
Tucson Greyhound Park

"Taking bets as low as $.10 and serving $1 beer is what it took for the Arizona Greyhound racing circuit to offer patrons a competitive and affordable sporting and gambling experience." (w/ Business Mail)

"The industry was forced to rely on these tactics, and substantial tax exemptions provided to them by the state, in order to survive the damage done to their industry by two decades of animal rights lawsuits and abuse accusations." – Doug Ducey, Governor

"Beginning in 1990, the first of these lawsuits were launched after animal rights activists invaded the Yuma racetrack and a partnered kennel facility. The dogs were found emaciated, dehydrated, and still wearing their racing muzzles. Eighty greyhounds eventually perished." (w/ *OnTrack*)

"By 2008 the narrative had not changed and, fed up with the persistent pressure of interest groups, the Arizona Gaming Commission decided to launch an investigation into the treatment of the dogs. They reported that between the two remaining tracks 540 dogs were unable to perform." (w/ Wild)

". . . these dogs suffered broken necks, limbs, backs, and some suffered from general respiratory illness. These dogs lived in deplorable conditions, where facilities allowed for flea outbreaks and where dogs were housed in cages covered in blood, urine, and fecal material." (AGC *ann. rep.*)

"The report's exposure of the industry's darker side would force the Phoenix track to close in 2009 and would later contribute to the closure of the Tucson track in 2016. For many, this report validated the fears that had long been presumed and exposed the grim conditions that were never considered." (w/ *AZ Pets*)

# Dinner with the Mayor

John's Travel Notes: An Introductory Course to Local Politics and *The Elected Official*

I sat down with the Chandler City Mayor, and his wife, and politely listened to *him* speak, for nearly an hour, about the personal benefits of a politician's lifestyle. Through it all, I couldn't understand if he was trying to convince me of something or convince me of nothing but either way, it worked—and I feel like I grew to know the man.

**CCM:** I am incredibly blessed to serve
[00:10:23]
**CCM:** my nation, my city, and my state.
[00:10:27]
**CCM:** I am incredibly blessed to be a part
[00:13:56]
**CCM:** of this wonderful community along with my wife
[00:14:00]
**CCM:** and beautiful daughter.
[00:14:05]
**CCM:** I am incredibly blessed to receive the support
[00:25:11]
**CCM:** of my voters and my party.
[00:25:16]
**CCM:** I am incredibly blessed to campaign in a district
[00:32:41]
**CCM:** that is welcoming to all races and genders.
[00:32:44]
**CCM:** I am incredibly blessed to have been afforded the opportunity
[00:45:51]
**CCM:** to maintain my position year after year—
[00:45:55]
**CCM:** but most of all, I am incredibly relieved
[00:46:01]
**CCM:** that my tenure has not attracted the eyes of the press.

# In Medina, Do as the Medinan
John's Travel Notes: An Introductory Course to Brutality

I've been sent north to spend the night with a Navajo family,
in their ceremonial hogan, and to speak with the progressive & *stunning*
queer artist Kenyan Lake.

I've been asked to perform a running ritual with them in the morning,
I haven't done anything like this in years.
I'm terrified.


[00:20:01]

**KL**: A boy was killed today in Yemen, by a provincial government,

**KL**: for indulging in his homosexuality.

[00:21:17]

**KL**: Finding the right words to speak about tragedy is hard to do

**KL**: while running.

[00:25:56]

**KL**: This family took me in when my own considered me a burden

**KL**: it's hard to find justice in this life.

[00:32:11]

**KL:** I wish I could have found the time to change the world

**KL:** it's hard to face it.

[00:45:31]

**KL:** I wish I could breathe life back into a body

**KL:** it's hard to find the time.

[00:56:24]

**KL:** I wish this boy had been given the chance to live his life

**KL:** it's hard to carry something like that in secret.

[01:32:17]

**KL:** I wish I'd learned to live properly before another one got away.

# "I've killed the Indian and built a white man in his place."
# — Rev. Thomas L. Moore

John's Travel Notes: An Introductory Course to Redemption

These words are painted, in horrifying commemoration, along the interior walls of the Yavapai County's Phippen Museum—their current exhibition, 'Remembering Our Indian School Days: The Boarding School Experience.'

The collection of artifacts: personals accounts, photographs, and essays, have all been compiled and curated by the county's Commission for the Arts in order to *preserve* the history of the Phoenix Indian School.

I've been invited to attend the opening ceremony
in order to reunite with Kenyan Lake and to speak with him
about his time spent there, in the late 70's and early 80's.


[00:10:01]

**KL:** By the time I attended the school

**KL:** it was voluntary.

[00:14:22]

**KL:** I learned to paint from a man who prioritized a *western* aesthetic

**KL:** and who believed my later work, especially my murals,

[00:15:01]

**KL**: portrayed, '*controversial scenes of Anglo-American aggression,*' and—

**KL**: represented, '*conservative depictions of my barbarous heritage.*'

[00:22:12]

**KL**: I was taught not to speak my language—and that wounded me.

**KL**: I was taught not to practice my religion—and that wounded me.

[00:26:51]

**KL**: I would like to be given the chance to recuperate my life.

**KL**: I wouldn't mind a little money.

[00:32:48]

**KL**: I want to sit back in an armchair and listen to my grandfather's stories.

**KL**: I wouldn't mind the silence.

# Percussion, Resonance
Sub: Your old [high]hat

John,

It seems that for a third time you are in desperate need of my *keeping-on-track* conversation. John, if this were a *day-time-series*—or a courtroom drama, then I would have dismissed you before our first commercial break:

John,

Your *manipulative, falsely-compassionate* persona has once again sullied your work. Your choice of pronoun, your "I," John, has opened the door to a whole host of issues, the least of them being an editorial bias. John, I need you to understand how your behavior impacts your office. Your words carry a great deal of weight—do not critique carelessly.

John,

You've attempted to explain some very deeply powerful and potentially harmful topics through the lens of your perspective; I need you to understand that other's words are not yours to manipulate. John, I believe you have genuinely crossed a line this time—please, please do not make me repeat myself again.

John.

Allen.

Allen Michael Power
Journalism Department Chair
Central Arizona Community College
allenp@centralaz.edu

# The Controversy Behind the New Fútbol Stadium
Civil Court Case 010116: The Tribal Action Committee vs the SRP-M Land Trust

"Last Thursday, a private consortium representing 17 unnamed valley businesses finalized the purchase of 37.1 acres of Salt River Pima-Maricopa land." (w/ *Phoenix Businesses*)

"The land-sale represented a coordinated effort between the tribal council and its local elders—the two groups hoped that the sale would revitalize their reservation and provide much-needed jobs and infrastructure to their vast and untamed territory." (w/ *Cowboys and Injuns*)

"The development was set to house the new Saguaro Lakes fútbol club and various high-market retail chains; however, the deal has quickly fallen apart. Facing multiple stays-of-appeal, courtesy of three civilian action groups, the developers, *Sun and Mortar LLC,* have pulled out of the project claiming, '[their] right to free and unencumbered practice was trod upon. . .'"

". . . and 'that if [their] commercial rights are not re-established under a new community bylaw, or tribal precedence, then [they] will be forced to *sue* the reservation for damages on the basis of breaching their contract.' —so, it seems that even in our *post-progressive* era there are still those who seek to impose a colonial sense of *will* on their economic activities." (w/ "Buying, Selling: The Profit")

# -Industry Partners-
*The Art of the Deal*, Chapter 21: Co-Authoring the Deal


"In 1994, after decades of cultivating and maintaining their 16,000-acre farming complex, the Ak-chin chose to break ground on a partnered, contemporary, gaming casino." (w/ *Recapping the Valley*)

"Negotiating with Nevada-based hotel and restaurant magnet, Caesars Entertainment Corporation, the tribe found an easy path to success in the Valley." (w/ Better Business Bureau *ann. rep. 1997*)

"Promising gamblers and resort goers a 'Vegas experience 330 miles south of Vegas' quickly helped fill the casino's seats and allowed their market share to rapidly grow."
(w/ *Letters and Numbers: Tourism*)

"As of 2018, the tribe has expanded their operation to include new community facilities, executive suites, restaurants, and a luxurious new golf course—which remains open to the public. . ."

". . . and although the Ak-chin only represent a small minority of the 65,000 staff members, which the Caesars organization currently employs, the Harrah's Ak-chin casino still provides its guests with the same exceptional, Caesars' experience."
(w/ *Hotels and  Hovels*)

# Terraforma: (N) The Great Hill of Northern Arizona
Research: Humphreys Peak / Seasonal Tourism

*The Setting:* "5 years of violence, on the slopes of the San Francisco Peaks, has left many in the sleepy, winter town of Flagstaff worn through—thin as paper." (w/ *Ironwood Chronicle*)

*The Conflict:* "Since the winter of 2013, the operating managers of the local skiing resort have opted to dump treated wastewater onto the mountain slopes in an attempt to manufacture artificial snow and extend the skiing season. (w/ *3 Nations News*)

*The Effect:* "Their venture has allowed the city to avoid seasonal depressions and has alleviated its dependence on the local college's student's spending; however, the move has alienated members of the tribal nations and has forced them to engage in destructive protests which jeopardize the city's improving economy." (w/ *Lou's*)

*The Fault:* "The tribes consider the Peaks to be an inheritable, sacred object which play an integral role in their oral history: Dook'o'oosłííd, the mountain which never melts—The mountain which made their land fertile." (w/ *The Lumberjack*: Local Points of View)

## Levity, Brevity
Sub: Your monotone

John,

I've noticed that your work has lost its music,
and I believe some recuperation is in order:
go find some.

I suggest you start online.
There are many local communities of listeners
that can point you in the right direction.

Stick to your tastes.
Write something that you're proud of
and proud to represent.

John,

Consider this a *for fun* assignment.
Get back in touch with yourself.

Allen.


Allen Michael Power
Journalism Department Chair
Central Arizona Community College
allenp@centralaz.edu

# A Rational Discussion of the Phoenix Punk Rock Scene
Revival, Maintenance, and Stability

"After releasing their sophomore effort, 'Revival, Maintenance, and Stability,' the preeminent Phoenix based punk rock group, Get-in-Get-Pregnant reclaimed their lofty position within the local punk scene & music charts." (w/ *Broadcast*)

"The super group, consisting of members from the mid 90's punk bands - Joe and Stacy, Guzzard, and the Senator's Milk Maids - chose to once again rock the central Valley and produce a challenging collection of music." (w/ KJZZ)

"Front-man, Paul Di claims their recent work '[should] be considered a representation of what's to come from the Valley scene,' but with their lyrics ranging from total political upheaval to more mellow and comedic tracks like, 'I'm in the Icebox'—we can't know what to expect. . ."

". . . however, what we can glean from their *press release* is that the album is meant to project a clear and direct anti-Californian/ anti-gentrification message (emphasizing home-grown, radicalized movements which champion regional superiority and a distinct southwestern identity.)" (w/ *Touring*)

# Marketing 101 – Capital Investment Among Other Sorts
Sub: Securing Sponsorships—Finding Us Friendly Advertisers

John,

I was impressed by how quickly and *effortlessly* you were able to carry out my suggestion; however, some recent clerical concerns have taken precedence over your *recovery*. It's been brought to my attention that you have yet to secure a reliable pool of committed investors or advertising clients for the *'Get-a-way's* upcoming issues. These advertisers are vital to the longevity of our operation, John—this oversight will not be tolerated. I implore you to contact the following organizations and to work with them to find some folks who would be interested in supporting us:

The Horace B. Griffen Trust and Estate Endowment:
Horace was a committed servant of the people
and worked as a Journalist for *The Arizona Republic.*
To honor his memory, his endowment's board of trustees
have given generously to independent media organizations
and should be more than willing to help us float our overhead.

The Pinal County's branch of the Better Business Bureau:
the bureau should be able to open the door to many of our local commercial businesses; they should be able to put you in direct contact with their ownership groups. Yet be warned, the bureau may be rather cliquey and abrasive at first. It's a *boy's club* down there.

Finally, the Phoenix trade show: speak with family-oriented start-ups
and other local small-craft businesses—encourage them
to consider the *commercial benefits* of an editorial
advertisement.


John,

Please find the companies and the people
who you want to represent and who
will complement our issues' various narratives.

Good Luck,

Allen


Allen Michael Power
Journalism Department Chair
Central Arizona Community College
allenp@centralaz.edu

# Horace B. Griffen Trust—Application for Financial Aid Disbursement

**Central Arizona Community College**
8470 N Overfield Rd
Coolidge, AZ, 85128
jrwhenn@centralaz.edu

Dear Rev. Michael-Thorpe,

I am writing you on behalf of the College of Journalism, and its student magazine *The Arizona Get-a-way,* in order to seek full or partial tuitional support for the upcoming fall semester.

Your foundation's monetary gift will help support an additional *faculty* position and will grant our student editors the capability to run our magazine unaligned for an additional (3) months.

Your foundation's contribution will allow our students the opportunity to continue their formal education and will allow us to continue to provide our community with an investigative outlet for local news.

Your foundation's support is gravely needed in a climate which discourages liberal arts spending in schools and which disregards independent publishing companies as *popularist* media.

I hope your foundation will review my case and my group's mission. I hope your foundation still believes in the benefits of written journalism, and I hope your foundation will consider my plea on the behalf of my community.

Thank you,

John Whenn

# The Crippling Letter: Opportunism
Re: Securing Sponsorships—Finding Us Friendly Advertisers -(2)-

Allen,

I met with the Better Business Bureau,
just as you suggested—they were warm to me at first,
but recoiled entirely when I mentioned your name.
They suggested that I pursue all future introductions
on my own and without tossing *your* name around.

So, without their help, I'm going to try my luck at the Phoenix trade show
and to be honest, I feel much less intimidated by the prospect of
interviewing a variable gaggle of casual start-ups than by entwining myself
with some more *established* and commercialized endeavor.

Cheers,

John


John Ryan Whenn
*Arizona Get-a-way Junior, Faculty Editor*
Central Arizona Community College
jrwhenn@centralaz.edu

# The Crippling Letter: Opportunism
Re: Securing Sponsorships—Finding Us Friendly Advertisers -(3)-

Allen,

I am not a man who enjoys being proved wrong.
The businesses which I interviewed at the show were well established
and represented real avenues to success for their young entrepreneurs—
it seems some minds are working well out west.

The folks I spoke to seemed to almost gleefully accept my offer
to run ads for them but recoiled entirely when I mentioned the cost.
However, in order to showcase these budding businesses—and to stick to
your demands—I've decided to perform a service for them;
I'm going to advertise their businesses at cost. I've decided to publish a
string of editorials about these young *marketmen* and women
and have vowed to charge them a standard 10¢ a word.


John Ryan Whenn
*Arizona Get-a-way Junior, Faculty Editor*
Central Arizona Community College
jrwhenn@centralaz.edu

II

# Organizers Weekend: Commercial Parity
Re: Securing Sponsorships—Finding Us Friendly Advertisers -(4)-

John,

I've been asked to concede my position and allow you the opportunity to pursue your *charity work*; however, if your plan is to simply patron the businesses which you perceive to be *primarily* emblematic of the Southwest, then I urge you to reconsider *your* position. I would suggest instead that you focus on broad topics which coincide with our conceptual theme: *Agency*. John, I believe you possess the talent to succeed in this crusade but may lack the intuition. Please consider the following topics as *launching points* for your editorials:

Focus on identity and identity politics. Consider sex, gender, class, and locality. Discuss the Southwest in "inclusive terms." Do not be afraid to invite *provocative* figures to apply for your *charitable* services.

Discuss the issues surrounding clean and accessible water. Consider the different communities which go with and without the resource. Work to portray an accurate examination of the industry and its inner mechanisms.

Invest in our local culture. Discuss food options, restaurants. . . or *guerilla groups* which pique your interest as a writer. Concern yourself with the *politics* of local businesses. Support our local businesses and their pursuits.

John,

Do not embarrass your *constituency* and do not make a fool of me.

Allen.

Allen Michael Power
Journalism Department Chair
Central Arizona Community College
allenp@centralaz.edu

# "A Girl's Political Window"
Paid for by Lippy Leinart for Governor


An order came across my desk this morning to interview our Democratic Gubernatorial candidate, Lippy Leinart:

I've been informed that she hails from Tucson, and that she's chaired the city's Commission for the Arts, as vice-president, for last 17 years. She's supposed to be the largest pop-culture icon that *Tucson* has ever produced.

**LL:** I'm sure your first question is, 'where could I have found the time
[00:00:10]
**LL:** to be a mother-*a working-mother*-and a politician
[00:00:13]
**LL:** in between my daily commitments and their inevitable chaos'—
[00:00:17]
**LL:** and my answer is, 'I just did.'
[00:00:20]
**LL:** I'm sure your second question is, 'where does my husband
[00:00:24]
**LL:** place in my own hierarchical flow chart of womanly tasks,
[00:00:29]
**LL:** marital duties, and motherly affection'—
[00:00:33]
**LL:** and my answer is, 'wherever he chooses.'
[00:00:35]
**LL:** And I'm sure your third and final question is, 'well, how does your bi-
[00:00:39]
**LL:** sexuality impact your voter's opinion or, how has your bi-
[00:00:41]
**LL:** sexuality come to define you as a candidate'—
[00:00:43]
**LL:** and my answer of course is, 'however I choose it to.'

# Katherine's Law
Paid for by The Schwitzman Law Offices

*The Setting:* "Preceding her dismissal, Mrs. Diana Hoffman-Këter worked for 9 years as an erotic masseuse and sexual escort for the Mindi's Massage Parlor in Glendale, Arizona." – Jim Schwitzman, *Esq.*

*The Conflict:* "During her termination, Mrs. Hoffman-Këter was required to pay '*reparations*' which parlor owner Gloria LeGuin stated, '*were standard procedure and were meant to cover lost revenues.*'" – Jim Schwitzman, *Esq.*

*The Complaint:* "Mrs. Hoffman-Këter believed that in her position she was considered a '*free and independent contractor*' and believed that under current Arizona law, she could not be targeted with '*hidden fees and termination expenses.*'" – Jim Schwitzman, *Esq.*

*The Fault:* "The court would side in favor of Mrs. Hoffman-Këter. The court found LeGuin in violation of Katherine's Law: an antidote to '*predatory pimps*,' which guarantees sex workers protection and representation in cases which exhibit abusive, monetary or sexual bondage." —Jim Schwitzman, *Esq.*

# The Franchise and the Franchisee
Finding the Prada Needle in the Haystack

"Now that a generation of entrepreneurs face commercial property listings as high as $2.8 million, the simple conclusion for the intelligent investor must be '*find the brands that find the money in the market.*'" (w/ Foodies & Roomies)

"Due to a century of compounding inflation and decades of expansive estate construction, the north Scottsdale real estate market has morphed into a manufactured '*buyers club of exclusivity*' which '*services the garish lifestyles of the incredibly rich. . .*'"

". . .It is this reputation that has drawn many in the Valley to condemn Scottsdale; yet, it is this reputation which has brought the lap of luxury to the Scottsdalian middle-class— '*it is this reputation which brought Gucci and Prada to the City Mall.*'" (w/ *White-Hot-Cowgirl Nights*)

"Scottsdale's current retail market resembles a miss-mash of brand loyalty—a battlefield of *exclusivity* and *civility*. Yet, when we really examine this chaos, we find '*a unity that is unbroken by economic boundaries and perceptions of class.*'" (w/ *Fashion Square*)

## *"Ride-Sharing Litter"* — Jeff Whitehall
Sun Valley Tribune, "Yellow Bikes: Grave Disaster or the Great Mobilizer?"

"Phoenix, Mesa, and Tempe
represent the future of *entrepreneurial
oversight* and systematic mismanagement." (w/ *Phoenix Businesses*)

"Phoenix, Mesa, and Tempe
represent overzealous attempts to enter
and corner the *Pay as You Go* pedestrian market." (w/ *Western Entrepreneur*)

"Phoenix, Mesa, and Tempe
represent the *abuse* of good faith, common property,
and consumer obligations." (w/ *Western Highlight*)

"Phoenix, Mesa, and Tempe
share the common and unsightly problem of abandoned and inoperable
*rent-and-ride* bicycles." (w/ Sun Valley Tribune)

# A Hippie in the Southwest
John's Travel Notes: An Introductory Course to the Northern Metropoles

A hippie in the *Southwest* would find the northern part
of our state to be an ideal place to lay down their head for an evening
or more. The largest northern cities, Flagstaff and Sedona,
boast tolerant atmospheres and market themselves by their many
natural retreats and holistic shops and businesses.
The two seem to be a breeding ground for the strange and the eccentric,
and that only seems to fuel the local identity. Visitors who are curious
about accommodations should be sure to call ahead to the Arizona
Department of Tourism at (602) 364-3700 where they will receive
detailed information about lodging and local points of interest.

## "Jerry might have liked to read what you've written." – Lois Jacka

John's Travel Notes: An Introductory Course to the Jacka Estate

I've been sent up north, to the rim of the pine ridge,
to bother the widow Jacka into parting with a few examples
of her late husband's work. I've been asked to purchase
a varied selection of Jerry's photos, namely those which conflate
regional *sectarianism* and the belief that all *men* are created equal:

**LJ**: You know John, I'm not sure if Jerry ever took anything
[00:10:01]
**LJ**: that could fit inside that very narrow pocket of yours;
[00:10:06]
**LJ**: he was very interested in traditional, indigenous portraits, yes,
[00:10:11]
**LJ**: but his main focus was the stunning landscape of the southwest.
[00:10:14]
**LJ**: Jerry made a name for himself because he took the time
[00:10:19]
**LJ**: to learn how to balance his own artistic desires
[00:10:21]
**LJ**: against his *canvas*. Jerry took his time to avoid creating defining
[00:10:24]
**LJ**: borders in his work. Jerry wanted his work to have integrity—
[00:10:27]
**LJ**: Jerry wanted people to see the world with as much *lightness*
[00:10:30]
**LJ**: and clarity as possible. Jerry loved this place and all he ever tried to be
[00:10:34]
**LJ**: was honest with it.
[00:10:36]
**LJ**: I'm sorry, John, I don't think I can help you.
[00:10:40]

# Quality Control: "What is Water and where does it come from?"
John's Travel Notes: An Introductory Course to Watering the Grass©

"Will the effects of Global Warming eventually provide Arizona businesses, farms, and residents with more reliable sources of clean drinking water?" – Sean Alexander, age 17.

Sean,

Thank you for submitting such a timely and interesting question: though my response may lead you to believe that this issue has more than one *correct* answer, I don't mean to dissuade you from conducting your own research and coming to your own *personal* conclusion—as mine may be little more than a *comb of the surface*.

Since 1901, the national branch of the Environmental Protection Agency has charted each metric which pertains to the volume rain which falls within the continental United States, and through their annual report, the organization has been able to record a steady, incremental growth of 0.17 inches per decade. That means that since 1901 rainfall within the broad borders of the United States has increased by nearly 2 inches on average (1.989in).

However, this data comes with some caveats: the Southwest, unlike the majority of our country, has lost nearly 20-30% of its annual rain fall due to our nation's shifting weather patterns. Now, that doesn't mean that the Southwest is facing terminal droughts in its future—it just means that most of the water consumed in the Southwest may eventually be purchased from other wetter and more seasonally rich states in the north, where annual rain fall has increased by an additional 20-30% over the same period.

[cont.]

Ia.) and although the desert's water resource is anything but secure and is in fact facing noticeable, annual declines there is still some hope left for the Southwest: for example, this year the Tucson, Kingman, Yuma, and Flagstaff stations recorded their highest rain fall since 1989 and the Phoenix Metro station recorded its first minimal loss or reduction since 2004.

So, Sean,

It seems the only answer, which I can truthfully give, to your question is, "we'll have to wait and see."

Cheers,

John Ryan Whenn


John Ryan Whenn
*Arizona Get-a-way Junior, Faculty Editor*
Central Arizona Community College
jrwhenn@centralaz.edu

# Watering the Grass©: Fountain Hills, The Water Conservation Project
Reducing, Reusing, Recycling—Recreationally

"Setting the precedent by relying entirely on treated sewage
for its operation, the Fountain Hills developer fountain and adjoining
water feature have helped pave the way for future estate developers in
Arizona to utilize our water resource for recreational purposes."
(w/ *Phoenix Businesses*)

"Since its construction in 1970, as a part of the city developer's plan
to entice homeowners to the area, the fountain at Fountain Hills
has provided the state with a *complementary* southern monument
and hourly entertainment." (w/ *Recapping the Valley*)

"Shooting gracefully 300 ft into the air, the fountain can be seen
from as far south as Mesa and as far east as central Scottsdale—
yet, when its operating at its maximum height of 560 ft, the fountain
can be seen from any vantage point in the central Valley."
(w/ Arizona Dept. of Tourism)

"The Fountain Hills developer fountain performs hourly
at a height twice the size of Old Faithful, and guarantees its travelers a
greater and more luxurious *viewing-experience*; currently, the fountain
straddles the local culture, art, and food of the Central Valley—
something that Yellowstone cannot hope compete with—and by day's
end the fountain simply leaves tourists and residents stunned
by its magnitude and its genuine, industrial sense of the Southwest."
(w/ *Yelp!*)

# Watering the Grass©: Marching Orders
Sub: Houghton Drilling Co. & Dry Canyon Estates -(1)-


John,

You seem to be stuck on the business side of *things*—
be warned, do not forget about the *individual* who consumes your work.

John,

Contact our network—find out from them what it takes to dig a well
and secure a modern homestead's *blue* water.

John,

What prevents our current pioneers from manifesting
their destiny? What's stopping Lady America's progress?
Why do we settle for our cities when we hear the desert
clicking her teeth and whistling?


Allen.


Allen Michael Power
Journalism Department Chair
Central Arizona Community College
allenp@centralaz.edu

---

# Watering the Grass©: Marching Orders
Re: Houghton Drilling Co. & Dry Canyon Estates -(2)-

Allen,

I'll consider this my reminder to perpetually serve.

John.

John Ryan Whenn
*Arizona Get-a-way Junior, Faculty Editor*
Central Arizona Community College
jrwhenn@centralaz.edu

# Watering the Grass©: The Conditional Surrender of Claim #46-01
Re: Houghton Drilling Co. & Dry Canyon Estates -(3)-

Dear Mr. Cunningham,

This letter is a reply to your recent request
to claim unalienable water rights over the spring at the far
end of your property.

I am writing you to inform you that your claim has been denied.
Your homestead and water rights have simply been established
too late in our system to warrant any legitimate ownership of the spring.

As you know, water rights in the state of Arizona are dispensed based
on what our legislature refers to as "first in time, first in right,"
and we believe that you have no legal right to any ground water
on your property.

Unfortunately, your spring had a claim assigned to it in 1975
and we are currently obligated to enforce that lessee's appropriated
ownership. However, if you can provide evidence which proves that the
claim has been unmolested for a period of 5 years or more then you may
resubmit your application (along with your proof) and we will reprocess
your claim.

Currently, your legal right to collect and retain rainwater (which falls within your acreage) will be granted to you; however, you are barred from establishing any underground storage or retainment of your water resource. <u>Please note</u> that any attempt to store or retain your water underground will void your right to the water.

If you have any questions, please refer to the bureau's bank of FAQ's.

Sincerely,

Jeff Hoyt

Dir. of Claim Management and Appropriation

# Watering the Grass©: Taken to Heart
Re: Houghton Drilling Co. & Dry Canyon Estates -(4)-

John,

Excellent work, you'll have to let me know
if our dear friend, Mr. Cunningham, gets his due—
I'll await your response with *baited* breath.

However, now that you've *entertained* your audience,
it's time for you to get back-to-business. John, a dear
friend of mine has alerted me to a developing story
about a recent sports drink fiasco; find out more, please.

Allen.


Allen Michael Power
Journalism Department Chair
Central Arizona Community College
<u>allenp@centralaz.edu</u>

-------------------------------------------------------------------------------

# Watering the Grass©: Taken to Heart
Re: Houghton Drilling Co. & Dry Canyon Estates -(5)-


Allen,

Of course, send me the link.

John.


John Ryan Whenn
*Arizona Get-a-way Junior, Faculty Editor*
Central Arizona Community College
jrwhenn@centralaz.edu

# Watering the Grass©: Salting the Earth, Sport Replenishment in the Sub-Tropic

*The Faucet*: The Piss Pipe, Paid for by the *Arizona Interscholastic Association*

"Finding that electrolytes are necessary for the body to metabolize its fats and to operate its muscle groups, we sought to create a product which would replenish our athlete's salts and preserve their competitive drive and physical prowess." – Tim Alexander, FighterFuel®

"Starting in the summer of 2017, all Arizona AIA-partnered facilities and leagues will be required to serve their athletes FighterFuel® during and after practice and are required to provide their players with the beverage before and after all scheduled game days. . ."

". . . Additionally, starting in the fall of 2018, all Arizona AIA-partnered facilities and leagues will be required to transition their arena and practice field sod to a synthetic Realturf® or a similar material. This requirement is meant to prevent the possible *bleaching* effects of saline-rich urine *provided* to us by our *male* athletes."
(w/ Arizona Interscholastic Association)

"Now, I'm no scientist, and I don't think you should quote me as one—but I've been drinking FighterFuel® and pissing in my yard since I was a boy and nothing's ever happened to me, my yard, or my parent's yard. I think this crusade is completely ridiculous. It's nothing but water and sugar, people."– Westley Haber, AIA Athletic Director

# // [34.5769° N, 113.1764° W]
John's Travel Notes: An Introductory Course to Local Traditions©

"If I grew up on a farm, and was mentally retarded,
Bruges might impress me." – Ray, *In Bruges*

I'm quoting, of course, from a movie
I adored as a young man; the plot of which often reminds me of the
strangeness I encounter lingering in this part of the world:

> To those residents who are new to the area, or to those of you who've recently decided to visit us during the *season-of-the-sun*, please prepare yourselves to witness a peeled and unseasonably-tanned *horde-of-the-living-dead* congregate at the check-out counters of CVS, Walgreens, Costco, and Target all summer long. – Kirk Pfotenhauer, "Hyperbole." (*Get-a-way*, vol. 41 pg. 42-56).

> While our state's-*more-timid*-individuals gather-*en masse*-in an effort to purchase _____ ~~remedies~~, others don religious garb; sleeveless-t-shirts, sunglasses, shorts, palm-oil, etc.,
> then flee their homes to graciously and *ceremoniously* serve as sacrifice to the altars of Boiling Heat and Powdering Sunshine. – John Whenn, "At Home In My Body" (*Get-a-way*, vol. 41 pg. 57-73)

# Local Traditions©: Make Sure You're Drinking Enough Water
Sub: // [34.5769° N, 113.1764° W] – Bagdad, AZ? -(1)-

John,

I noticed that your previous "critique" of our state's *summer-izing* citizens was based primarily on your belief that our readers possess an unfamiliarity with our climate and not based on any genuine *strangeness* you found hidden within the process. I think that it's time for you to stop discussing the issues which you find unordinary or otherwise foreign to our readers. My patience is wearing thin, John, and your work has yet to achieve the promises you made to me. For the remainder of your residency, I would like you to focus on the following:

Uniquely Arizonan or otherwise southwestern businesses: show me and the reader that you understand what I'm asking of you—show me that you understand what local business and regional autonomy means for the Southwest.

Discuss synergy and cohesion between infant organizations and their benefactors. Make me believe that you have done your research and that you have genuinely immersed yourself in the culture which you claim to be an authority of.

John,

I am not displeased with your work as a whole but you seem to be distancing yourself from our theme. I think you're *enjoying* too much freedom in your position and I believe it's time you reel it in.

Allen—

Oh, and while I have you—
make sure you're drinking enough water.
Your students have been worried about you.

Allen Michael Power
Journalism Department Chair
Central Arizona Community College
allenp@centralaz.edu

# Local Traditions©: Cactus Butter
Re: // [34.5769° N, 113.1764° W] – Bagdad, AZ? -(2)-


Allen,

First, I'm sorry that you feel that I've failed
in my mission to capture the Southwest
as *you* perceive it. I'll make a note to myself
and try to finish out my residency in a more *favorable*
light.

Second, thank you for your concern
about my fluid intake—
I purchased a sizable (& reusable) water bottle,
like many of my students suggested,
and sourced it locally too.

Finally, speaking of *thinking local,*
have you ever tried Cactus Butter?
I found a coupon online and ordered
some. I hope the taste isn't *too sharp*.

Cheers,

John


John Ryan Whenn
*Arizona Get-a-way Junior, Faculty Editor*
Central Arizona Community College
jrwhenn@centralaz.edu

# Local Traditions©: [Redaction] Cactus Butter
Re: DO NOT CONSUME CACTUS

Allen,

I believe I've fallen prey
to a decisively clever marketing
campaign:

> BUY 2 GET 1 FREE
> Online Only (BUY 1 GET 1 In Store)
> **Sweet Nectar Cactus Butter**
> Expires July 15

It occurs to me now
that what I have purchased is colloquially
referred to as Cactus Butter
but what is genuinely
our local delicacy, *Prickly-Pear-Jelly*.

I've been assured that it is completely safe.
Thank you for your concern.

Cheers,

John

John Ryan Whenn
*Arizona Get-a-way Junior, Faculty Editor*
Central Arizona Community College
jrwhenn@centralaz.edu

# My $20 Lunch with a Yuma County Sherriff
John's Travel Notes: An Introductory Course to Dining in the Desert©

My $20 lunch with a Yuma County Sheriff
started out with free coffee at the station
and ended $14.43 later at the Denny's
restaurant around the corner.

I took the liberty of keeping an itemized total
for those who would be genuinely interested,
or for those who are just simply fans of math:

Orange Juice - $2.00
Breakfast Sampler - $9.99
Black Coffee - $1.50
Tax - $0.94
Tip – $5.57

## Dining in the Desert©: PBS Frontline Exclusive, "The Business of Food"
Culture, Climate, and Citrus, paid for by PBS and viewers like <u>you</u>

"It is no secret that the North American household ranks amongst the richest households in the world, and because consumers can comfortably choose to spend less than 7% of their annual income on food; the average North American, adult consumer continues to retain their top spot on our list of *Wealthiest Eaters* in the world. . ."

". . . Even though these 'average adults' hardly compare to the *Wealthiest Eaters* in their own country (who spend less than 1% of their income on food), they stand heads above smaller nations like Kenya, Sudan, and Zimbabwe—where families often spend 40-60% of their annual income on meals and water. . ."

". . . Economic statistics like these are what drive hundreds of thousands of immigrants to the shores of the United States every year; yet, hidden behind these statistics are a multitude of thriving industries and businesses which cater exclusively to a 'lifestyle of preference,' a lifestyle rich in choice and guiltless spending: a life of sheer excess."
(w/ John Schur PBS Frontline)

"*Trial and Error*, the newest cookbook by esteemed Chef Laura Smoak from Scottdale, Arizona, is home to some wonderfully rich and experimental dishes which owe their heritage to the Southwest and to the multitude of cultures which reside there. Laura herself stated that her book's title is meant to enrich the cooking experience—and hopes to embolden those who would otherwise avoid cooking. . ."

"... Laura's dream is that all people learn to explore flavor and exotic delicacies through safe and friendly instruction and hopes that 'meal time' can finally return to the American dinner table.
Laura urges her readers on page 3, '[to] never give up, and [to] press on through adversity in the kitchen; *trial is error,* and you should think of your trashcan like an easel...'"

"... Laura paints a wonderful picture of the budding and burgeoning chef, yet, she does little to acknowledge the waste which she is openly encouraging or the rampant spending and acculturation. Laura envisions a future of food and harmony but does not consider the *side-effects* of her utopia. There are many people like Laura, here in the Southwest—many who abuse their privilege in the very faces of those who struggle to survive in stark contrast to their vast world of excess." (w/ *Table Manners*)

# Dining in the Desert©: Finding Ways to Cook for Two

The Jump-up-and-getcha'-some Rattlesnake, Paid for by Laura Smoak's *Trial and Error*

> **The Jump-up-and-getcha'-some Rattlesnake**
> *Start to Finish: 35-65 minutes*
>
> 1 cup (240 ml) buttermilk
> 1 Whole, skinned, rattlesnake
> 1 ½ Tsp (20 g) garlic powder
> 1/2 Tsp (8 g) onion powder
> 1 cup (120 g) all-purpose flour
> 2 Tbsp (30 g) corn starch
> 1 cup (240 ml) vegetable oil, for frying
> Dust with chili powder, to taste

Step 1: Prepare the snake. Let the meat soak in 1 cup (240 ml) of buttermilk for 30-45 minutes.

Step 2: Remove the meat from the broth and let it stand for 3 minutes.

Step 3: Mix the breading: Combine 1 ½ tsp garlic powder (20 g), 1/2 tsp onion powder (8 g), 1 cup (120 g) all-purpose flour, and 2 Tbsp corn starch (30 g) in a bowl; screen the mixture until it presents one homogenous color and texture.

Step 4: Heat the pan. Set the burner to high heat and warm 1 cup (240 ml) of vegetable oil in a shallow skillet or sauce pan.

Step 5: Separate the meat. Cut the rested meat into 1 ¼ inch sections and batter them with the flour breading.

Step 6: Fry the meat. Place the battered sections gingerly into the warmed oil and let them fry for 5 minutes.

Step 7: Serve the meat. Remove the battered sections from the oil once they've browned and plate them in an aesthetically pleasing pattern. Serve the dish with white sauce.

# Dining in the Desert©: The Banquet Challenge
*As it hurts, it heals*; paid for by The Arizona Philanthropy Group

"'Let's give this recipe some time to maturate—it should only take 10-15 minutes to achieve the texture we're looking for, but while I have you engaged, I would like to introduce to you the group which the proceeds of this evening will go to support...'"

"'... however, I would first like to thank our generous benefactors, the Arizona Philanthropy Group, for providing us with a space for this evening. Second, I would like to thank all of you for purchasing copies of my cookbook—your additional contributions have truly made this evening possible...'"

"'... Now, to the purpose of our evening. It is my goal that tonight's event and others like it will contribute to increased awareness and investment capital for the humanitarian organization, Sonoran Peoples Foundation. It is my hope that this evening provides these wonderful people with the financial and commercial support that they so dearly need...'"

"'... It is no secret that migrants suffer horrible, unspeakable, atrocities at the hands of their Coyotes and by mother nature herself, and it is no secret that the United States and her politicians have been less than remotely concerned about their well-being. In our current climate, the Sonoran Peoples Foundation remains the only friendly and prepared humanitarian organization in the region...'"

"'... Your donations tonight will go towards directly supporting their mission by funding their newly balanced *field rations*: 7 in total, all sporting collections of different food items and ready-to- eat recipes. Each contain selections of various vitamin supplements, iodine tablets, and most importantly traces of human kindness. It is your *privilege* to be able to fund an organization like this and I urge you to pressure your friends and their friends to consider supporting the SPF as well.'" – Laura Smoak (w. 48/50)

# Dining in the Desert©: The Last Meal, or the Humanitarian Option
The Troche Recipe, Paid for by the *Sonoran Peoples Foundation*

---

Field Ration #1
Consume as Directed (Comer Según las Indicaciones)

$\frac{1}{3}$ Cup of Whole Wheat Grains/ Kernels (Taza de granos de trigo integral / granos)
$\frac{1}{2}$ Cup of Dried Pinto Beans (Taza de frijoles pintos)
$\frac{1}{3}$ Cup of White/ Brown Rice Mix (Taza de Mezcla de arroz blanco / marron)
4oz of Dark Chocolate (Chocolate negro)
2oz Self-Serve Peanut Butter (Mantequilla de maní)
1 Whole Wheat, Pre-Portioned, Bread Loaf (Pan de trigo)
3 Iodine Tablets (Tabletas de yodo)
4 500mg Tylenol Tablets (Tabletas de Tylenol)
2 Claritin 24-hour allergy relief© (Tableta de Claritin)
1 Sanitary Alcohol Wet Wipe (Toallita húmeda con alcohol sanitario)
28 sheets Charmin Ultra Strong© (Hojas Charmin Ultra Strong)
1 box (16 ct.) Blue Diamond© Matches (Mechas de Blue Diamond)

May be consumed without water (Comer sing agua)

---

1. If water is available (please avoid standing water), use 2 cups (16 oz) to boil the mixed rice, wheat grain, and pinto beans. *Si, hay agua disponible (evite el agua estancada), usar 2 tazas (16 oz) para hervir el arroz mezclado, grano de trigo y frijoles pintos.*

2. If water is not available, discard the mixed rice and consume the wheat grain and pinto beans separately. *Si, no hay agua disponible, deseche el arroz mixto y consuma el grano de trigo y los frijoles pintos, por separado.*

3. Consume (4oz) Dark Chocolate, (2oz) Self-Serve Peanut Butter, and (1) Whole Wheat, Pre-Portioned Bread Loaf at your own pace; however, you are advised to portion these servings. *Consume (4 oz) de chocolate negro, mantequilla de maní de autoservicio (2 oz) y (1) trigo integral, porcionado, pan de pan a su propio ritmo; Sin embargo, se recomienda dividir estas porciones.*

4. Use Iodine tablets to treat suspect or unsanitary water (avoid drinking standing water). Use Tylenol and Claritin tablets as needed for pain

symptoms. *Usar tabletas de yodo para tratar el agua sospechosa o no higiénica (evite beber agua estancada). Usar tabletas de Tylenol y Claritin según sea necesario para los síntomas del dolor.*

5. Finally, good luck & welcome to America. *Finalmente, buen suerte muchachos, y bienvenidos al Estados Unidos.*

## jw2293@utah.edu

Sub: Horace B. Griffen Trust—Application for Financial Aid Disbursement

John,

It's taken me a while to track you down, now that you've left Coolidge. Allen tells me that you returned to Salt Lake to continue *creative* writing; I think that's the intelligent thing for you to do.

I am sorry that this response has taken longer than normal for me to generate, but I wanted to make sure that you were headed in a clear direction before I commented on your application:

---

---------- Forwarded message ---------
From: Michael Thorpe <mat22@gmail.com>
Date: Sun, September 4, 2016 at 8:12 PM
Subject: Horace B. Griffen Trust—Application for Financial Aid Disbursement
To: John R. Whenn <jrwhenn@centralaz.edu>

Dear Mr. Whenn,

Unfortunately, your recent application for financial aid did not *satisfy* our endowment's *recipe for success*; or, to state it plainly—your submission's appeal lacked amorality, John. Your submission's deflective, self-serving, and egotistical approach made it very clear to the board and to myself that by applying for this scholarship you simply meant to protect yourself and your office of employment from future financial hardship. At this time, we believe that your application was submitted with the intent to defraud; we consider your submission's classification of, '*student paper*' to be a grossly inadequate examination of what *you* intended to print during your summer as a *serial* columnist.

John, we consider ourselves to be a charitable organization and believe that you intended to take advantage of our generosity. Additionally, we believe that you intended to defraud your students of their education in order to service your own agenda. John, I personally believe that if you had been given the chance to publish your work with impunity, behind the label of a *student paper*, then you would've profoundly widened our community's already-deep cultural rifts. John, I believe that your work may provide the tools to *bridge-building* and rectification in the future, but presently I consider your work problematic, dangerous, and misleading. John, I do not take my rejection letters lightly; I believe my letters provide organizations with the onus to grow and to learn from their mistakes, and your case is no different.

John, life has dealt you an unfair hand—God has given you talent, but he has also made you very arrogant; please consider us again once you've grown and learned to incorporate a *greater* cast of characters.


Thank you,

Rev. Michael A. Thorpe

# About the Author

Connor Bjotvedt received his Master of Fine Arts in Writing from Spalding University. He was awarded the Charles E. Bull Creative Writing Scholarship for Poetry by Northern Arizona University where he received his Bachelor of Arts in English, Literature, and Creative Writing. Connor was a 2018 Pushcart Prize nominee and his work has appeared in *Rain Taxi, the Santa Fe Literary Review, the Haiku Journal, Three Line Poetry, catheXis Northwest Press*, and *The Wayfarer*, among others.

## About the Press

Unsolicited Press is a small publishing house in Portland, Oregon and is dedicated to producing works of fiction, poetry, and nonfiction from a range of voices, but especially the underserved. Our team has published books that aren't afraid to take on topics of race, gender, identity, feminism, patriarchy, mental health, and more. The team is comprised of hardworking volunteers that are passionate about literature.

Learn more at www.unsolicitedpress.com.

www.ingramcontent.com/pod-product-compliance
Lightning Source LLC
Chambersburg PA
CBHW030347100526
44592CB00010B/865